NEW BALANCE

Mindful Coloring

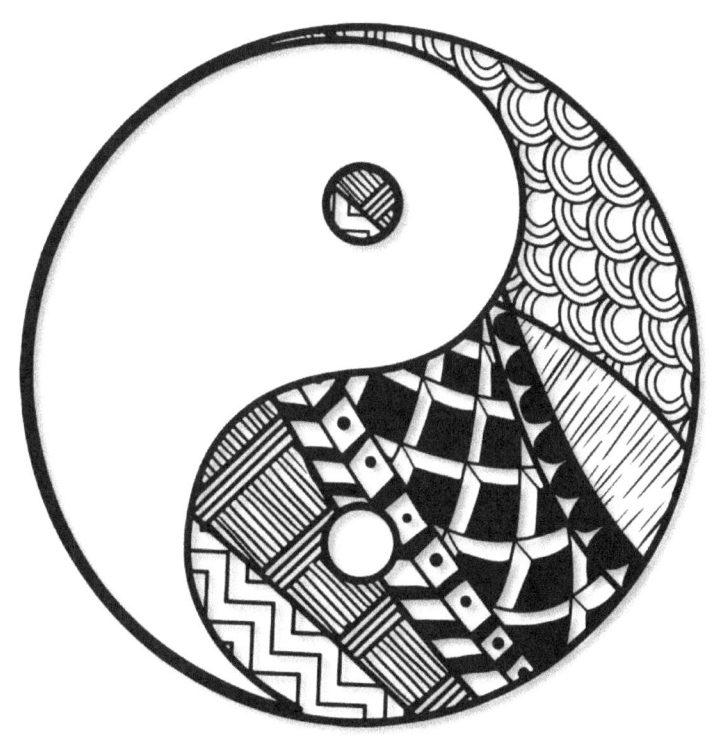

Adult Coloring Book

LG DESIGNS

This book consists of a series of intricate designs to help you find your inner peace through coloring.

The repetitive, symmetrical nature of these designs helps focus and calm the mind. Take your time coloring and allow yourself to focus inwardly.

Mindful coloring is all about being in the moment. Coloring is also an excellent way to increase your awareness.

There is no sequence to these patterns, and you can start anywhere you wish in the book. Just pick one that feels right to you now. Ask a question or think of an issue that's been bothering you; perhaps even write I down on the opposite side of the paper.

Begin by focusing on the colors you chose and the patterns you are going to color.

Appreciate the qualities of the moment and acknowledge any underlying feelings, emotions, or sensations.

You'll soon feel balanced and the answer will appear in you newly relaxed and refreshed mind.

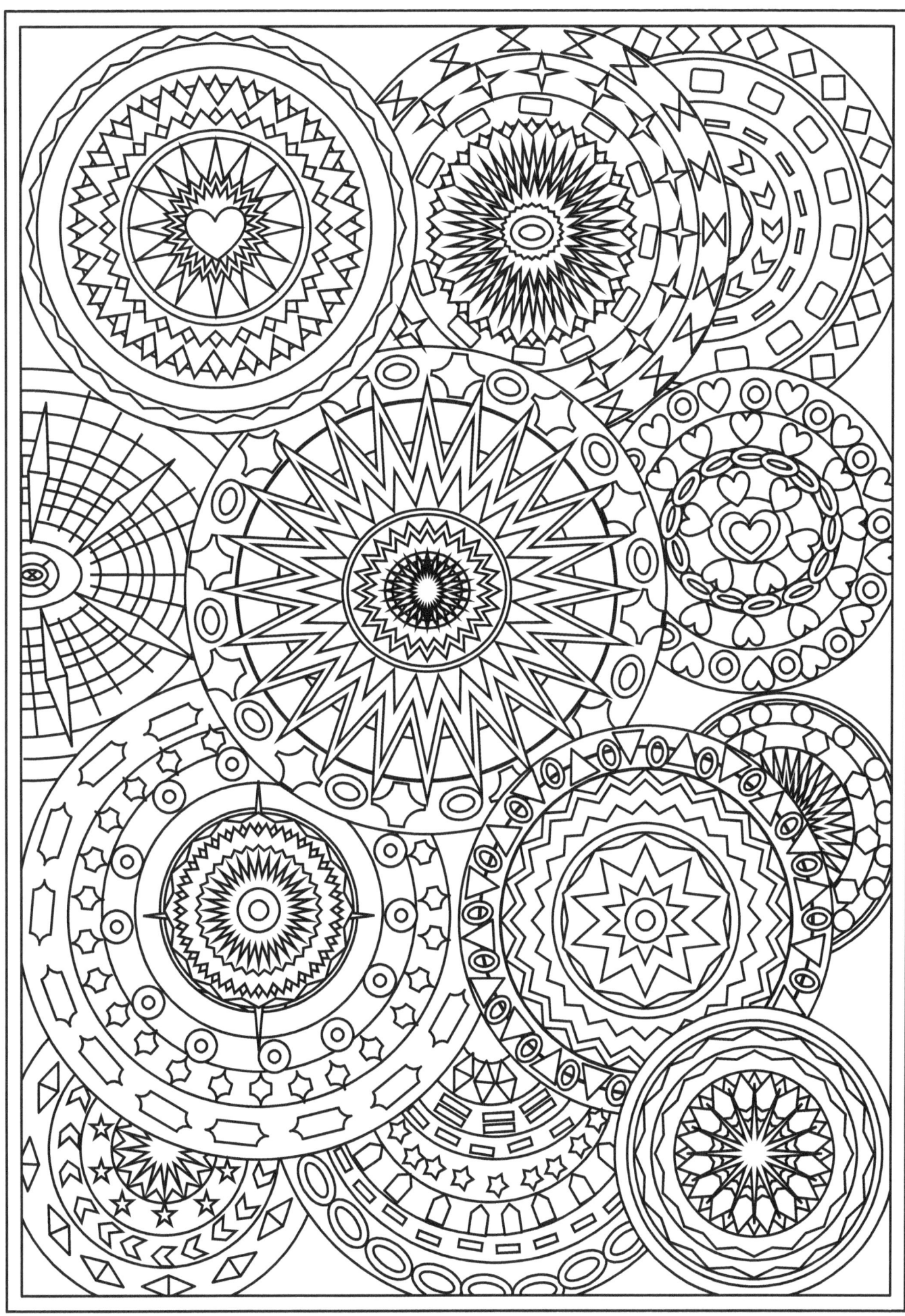

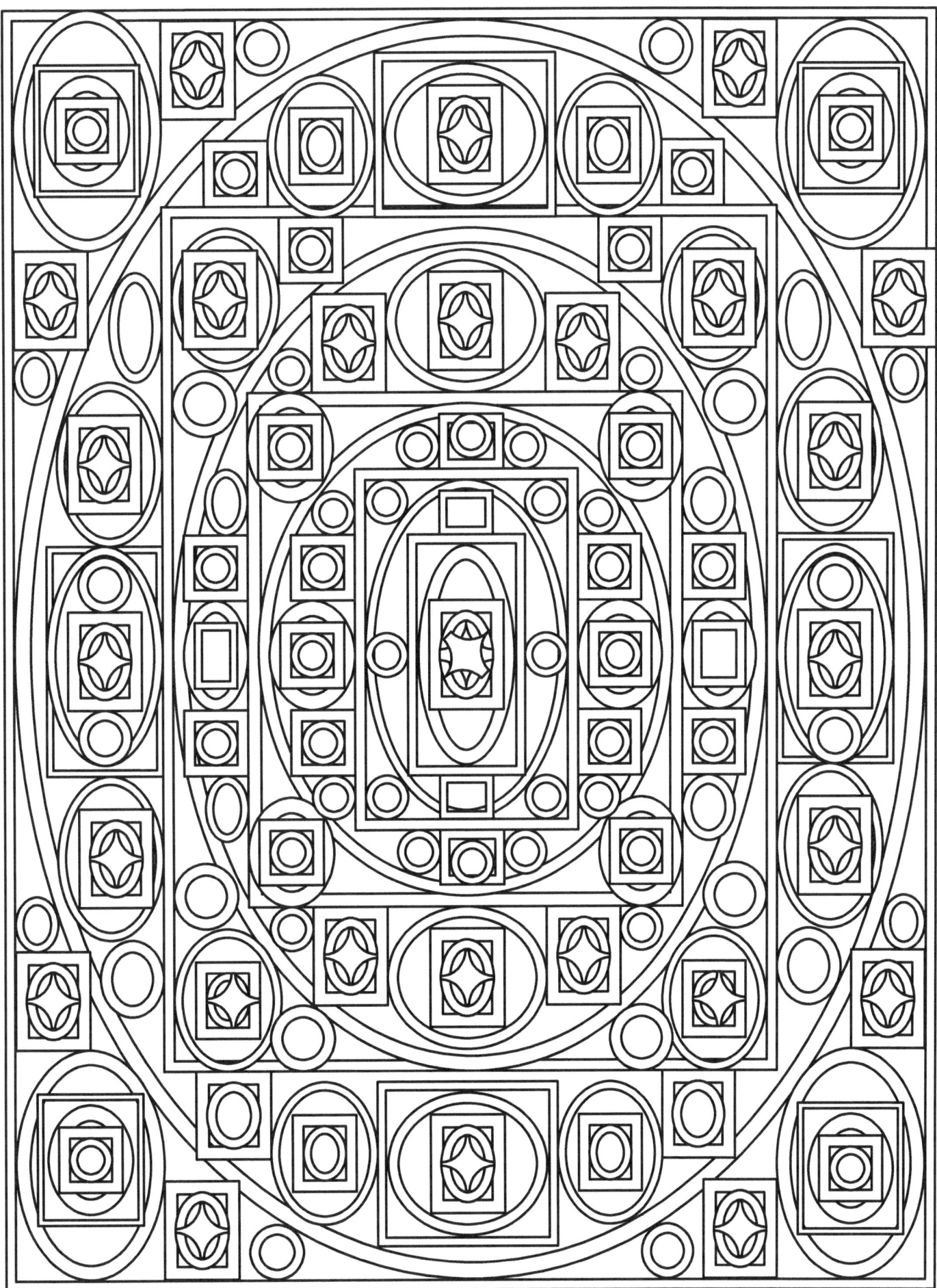

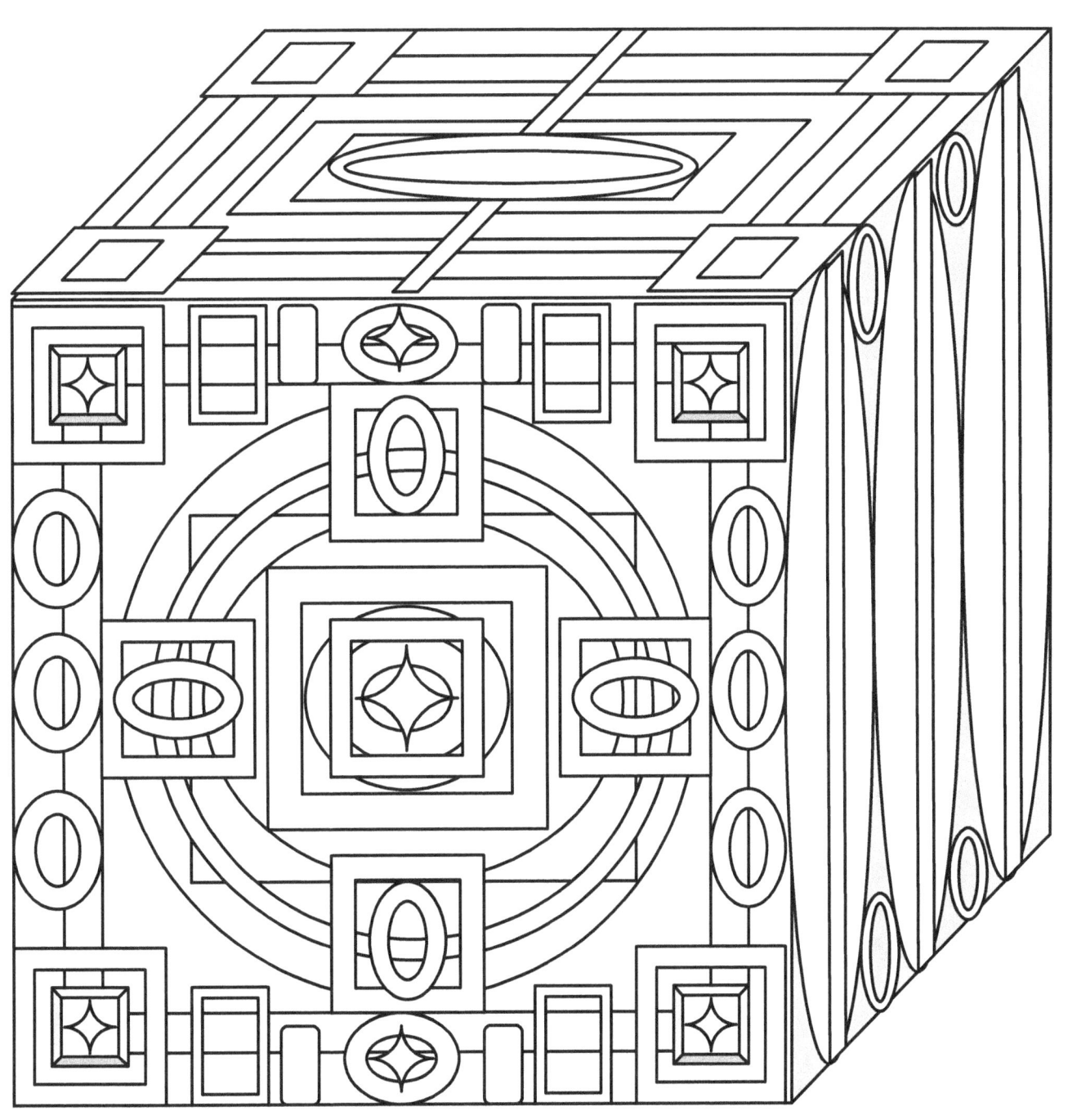

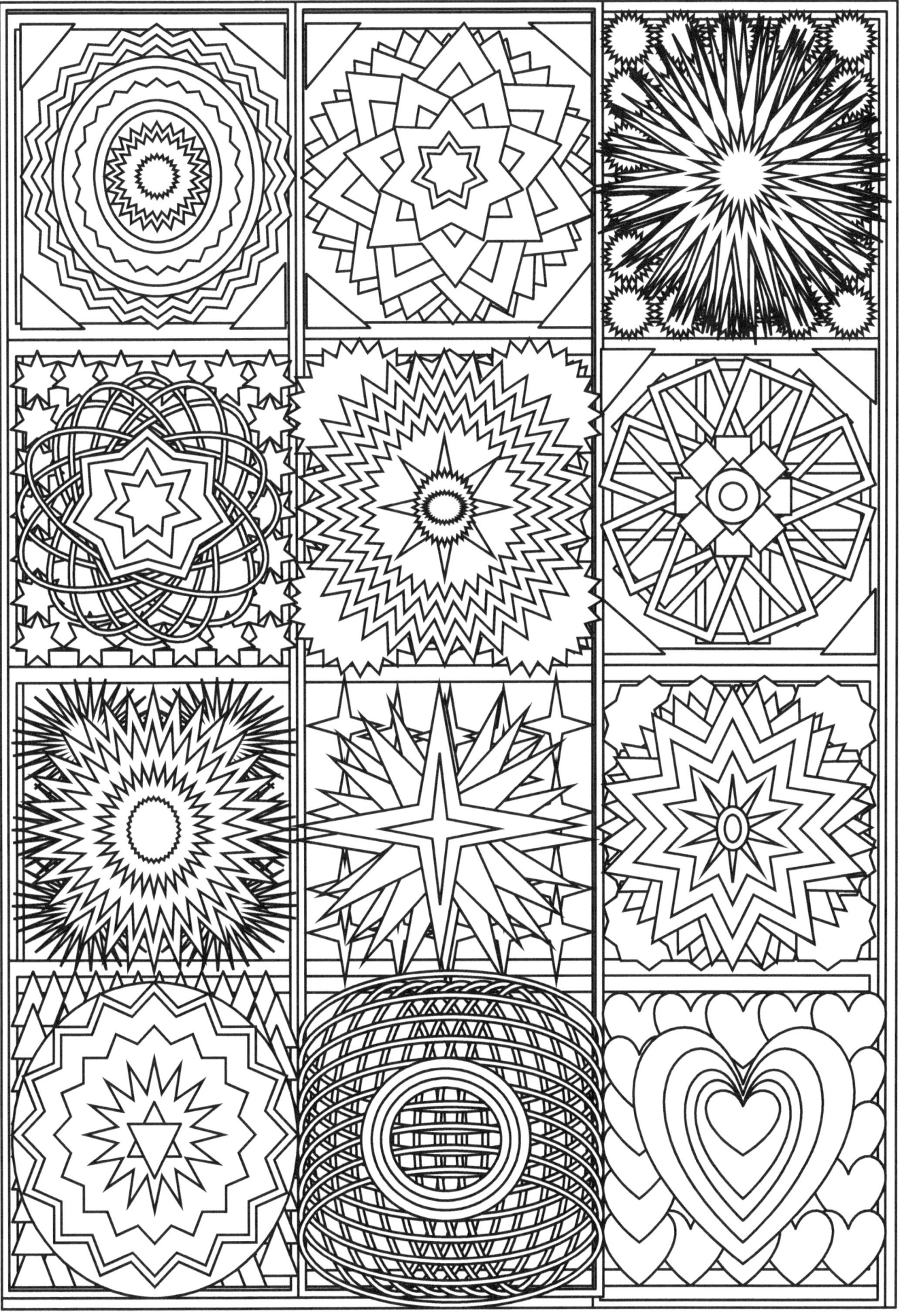

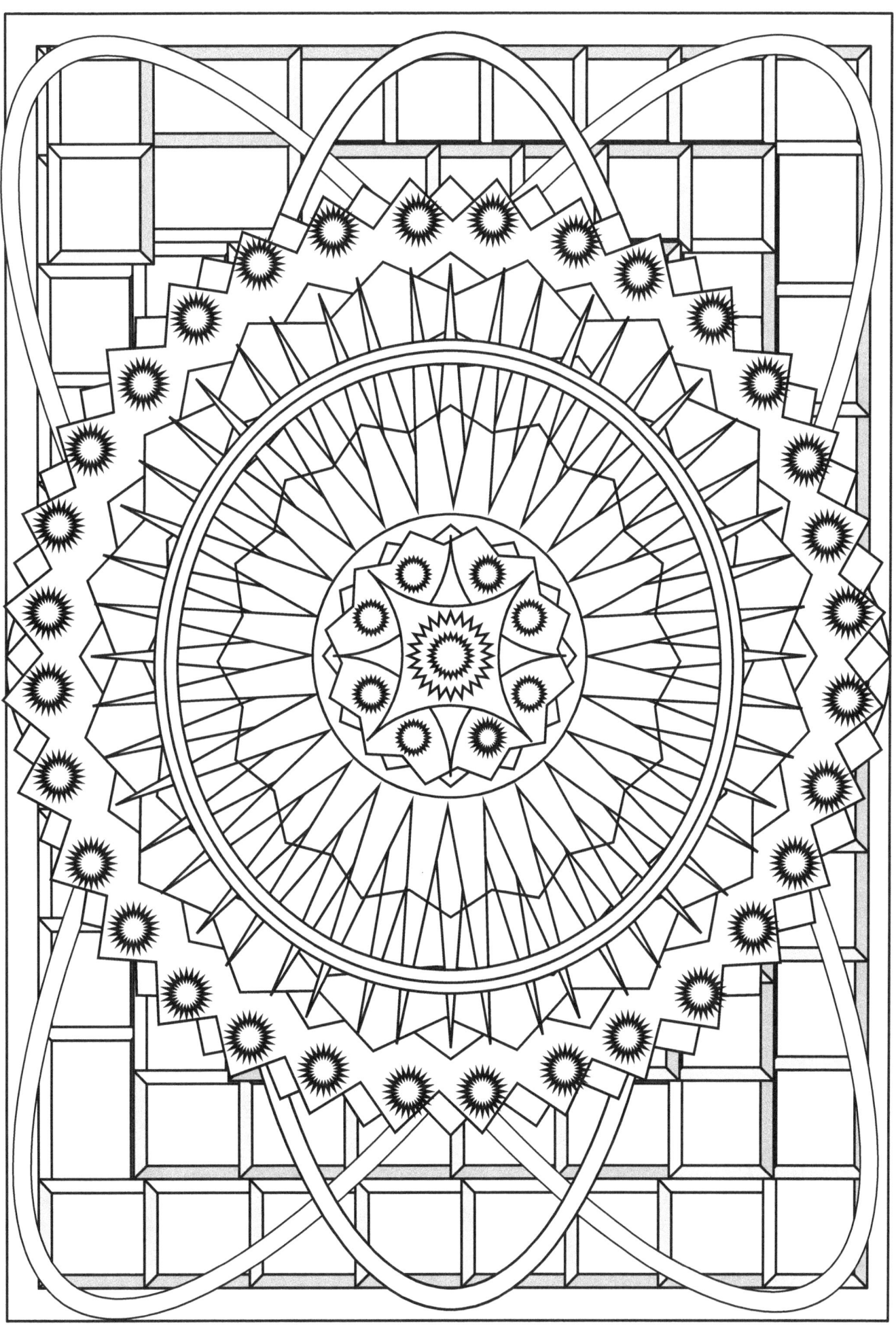

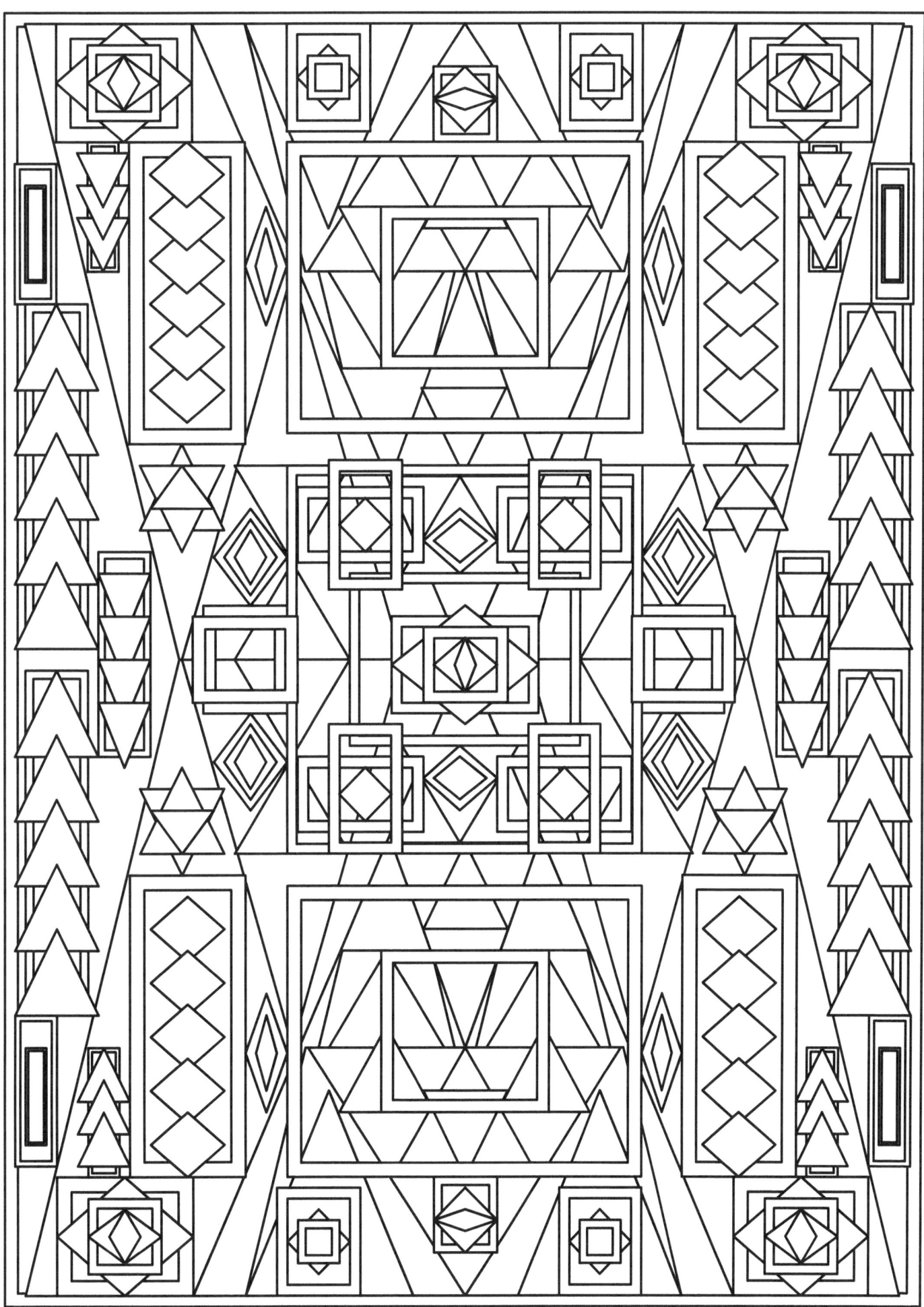

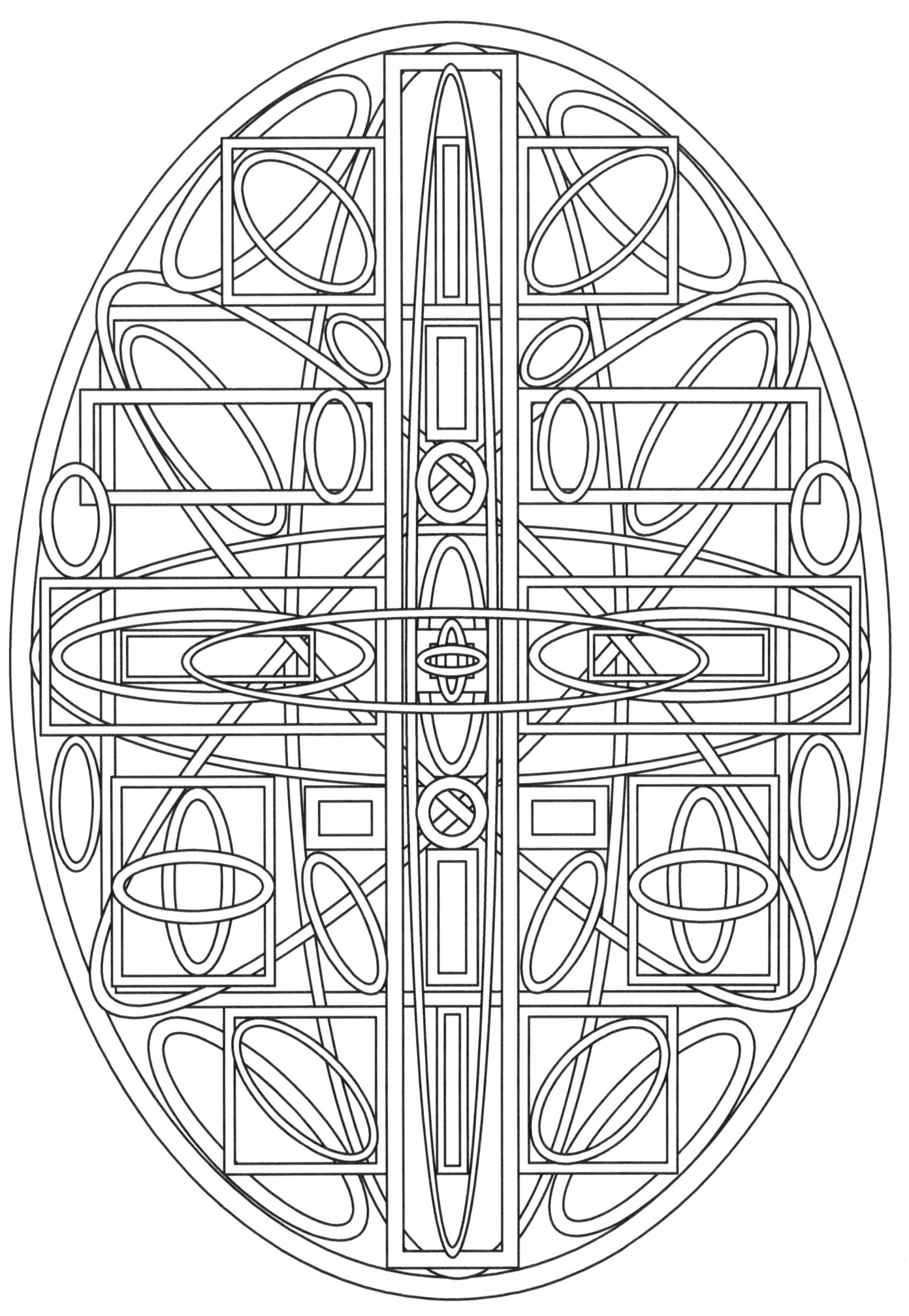

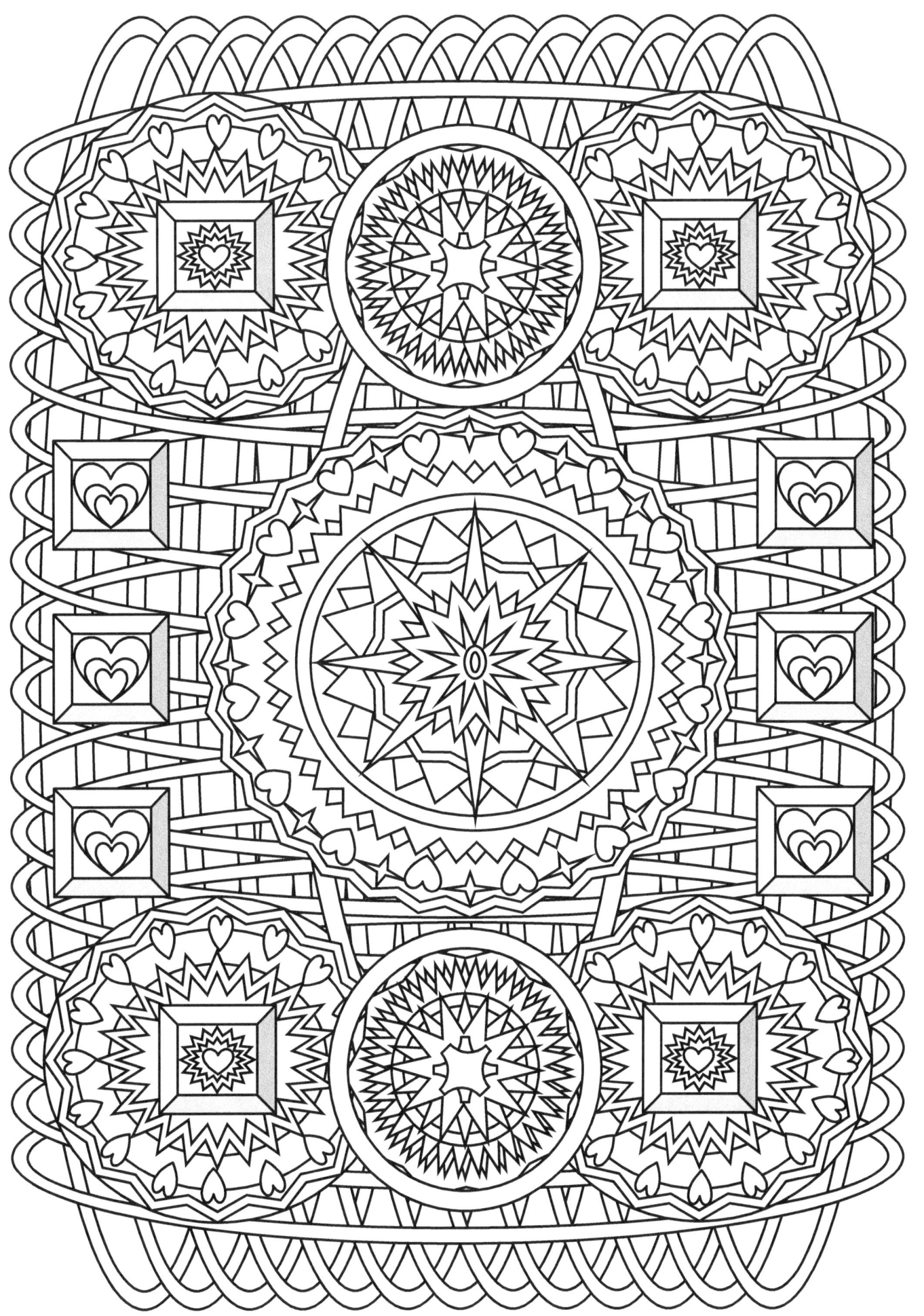

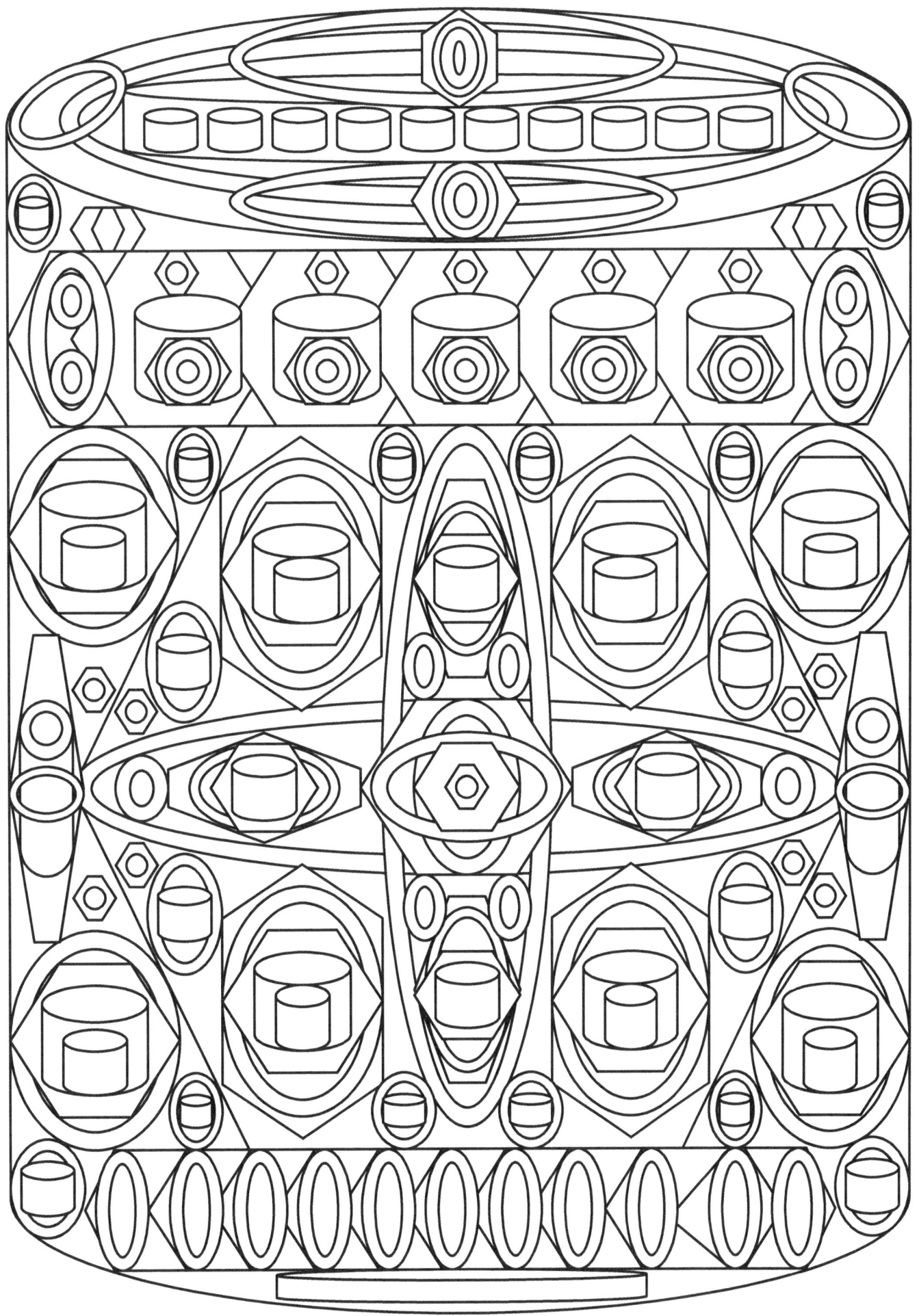

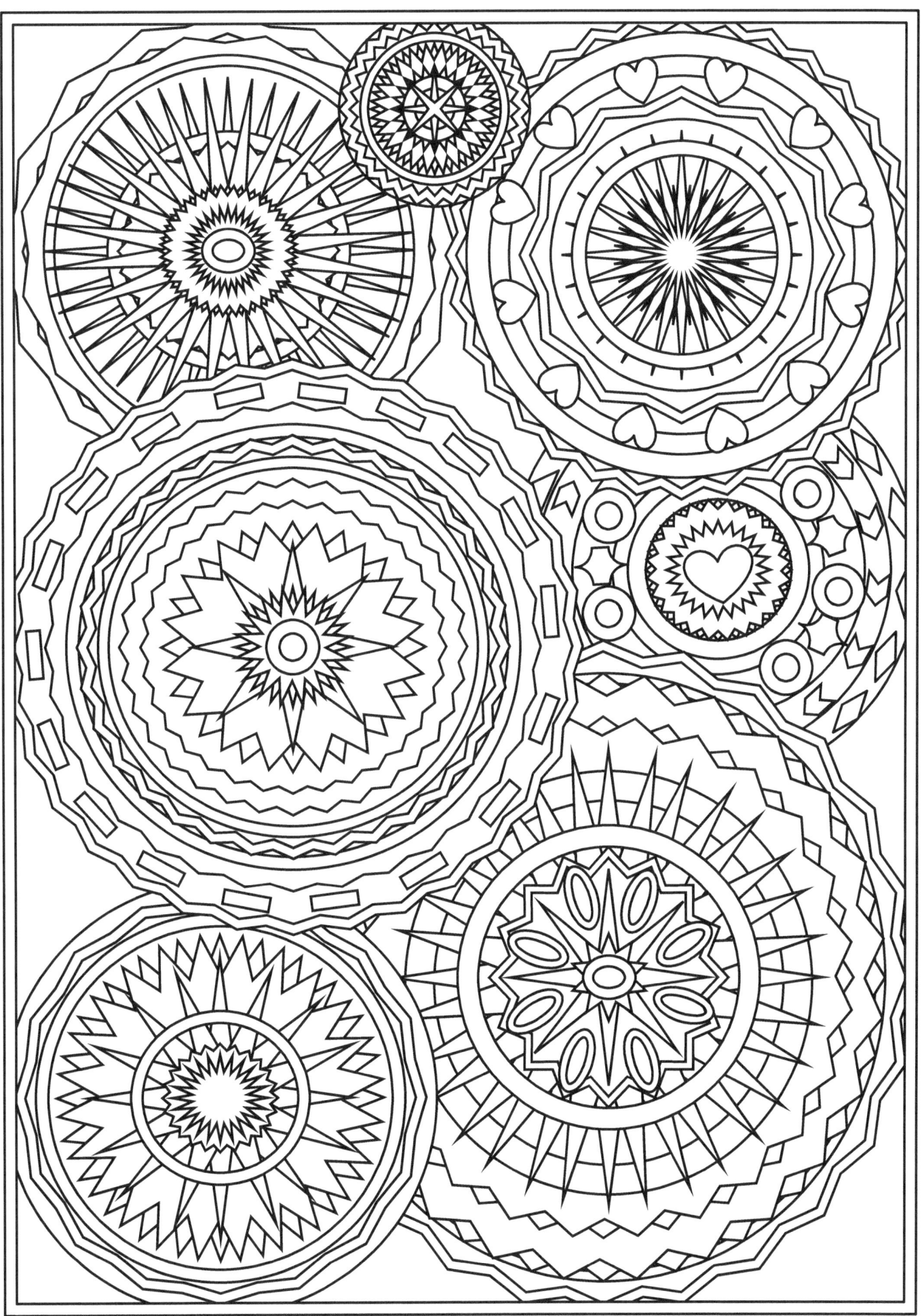

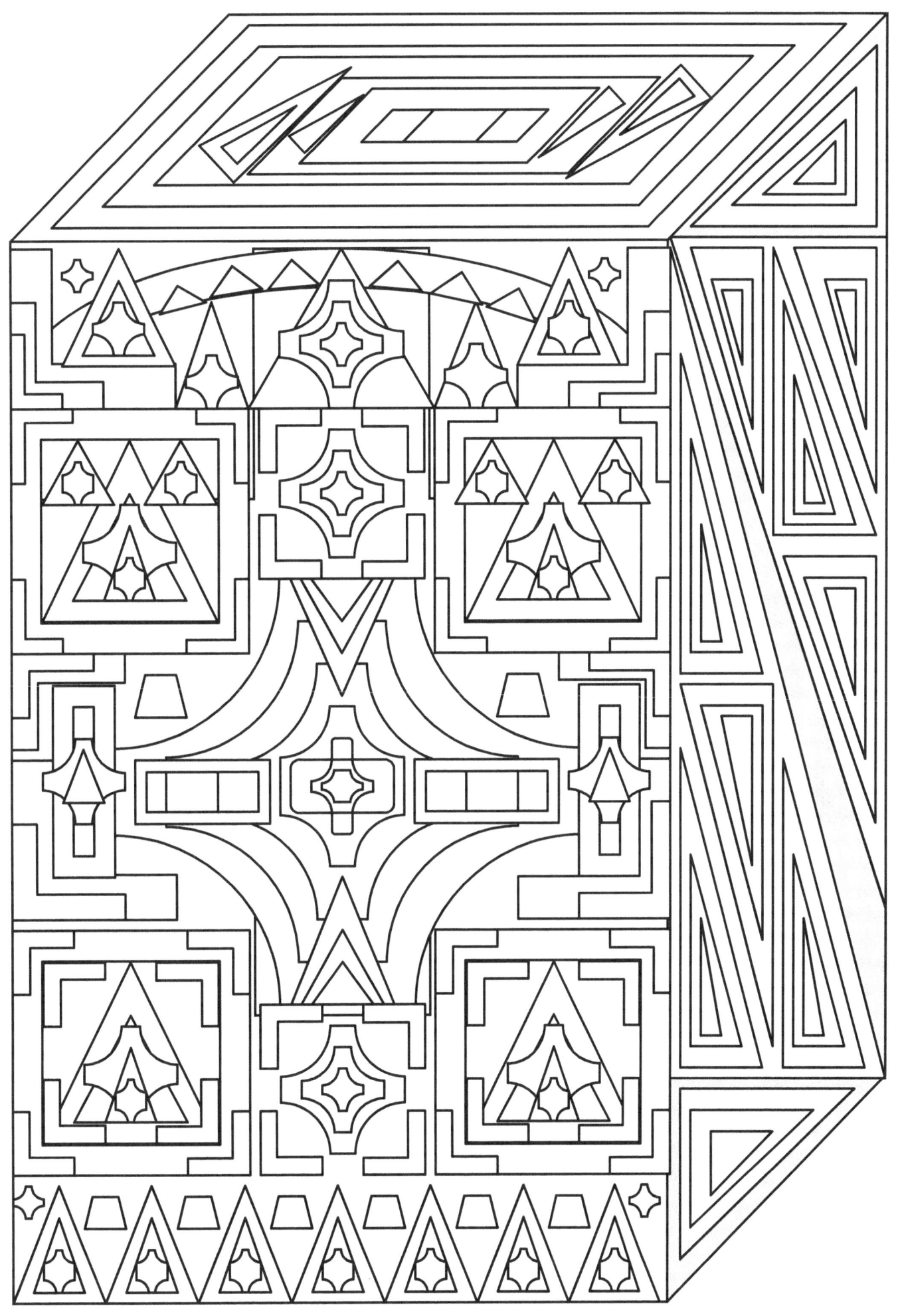

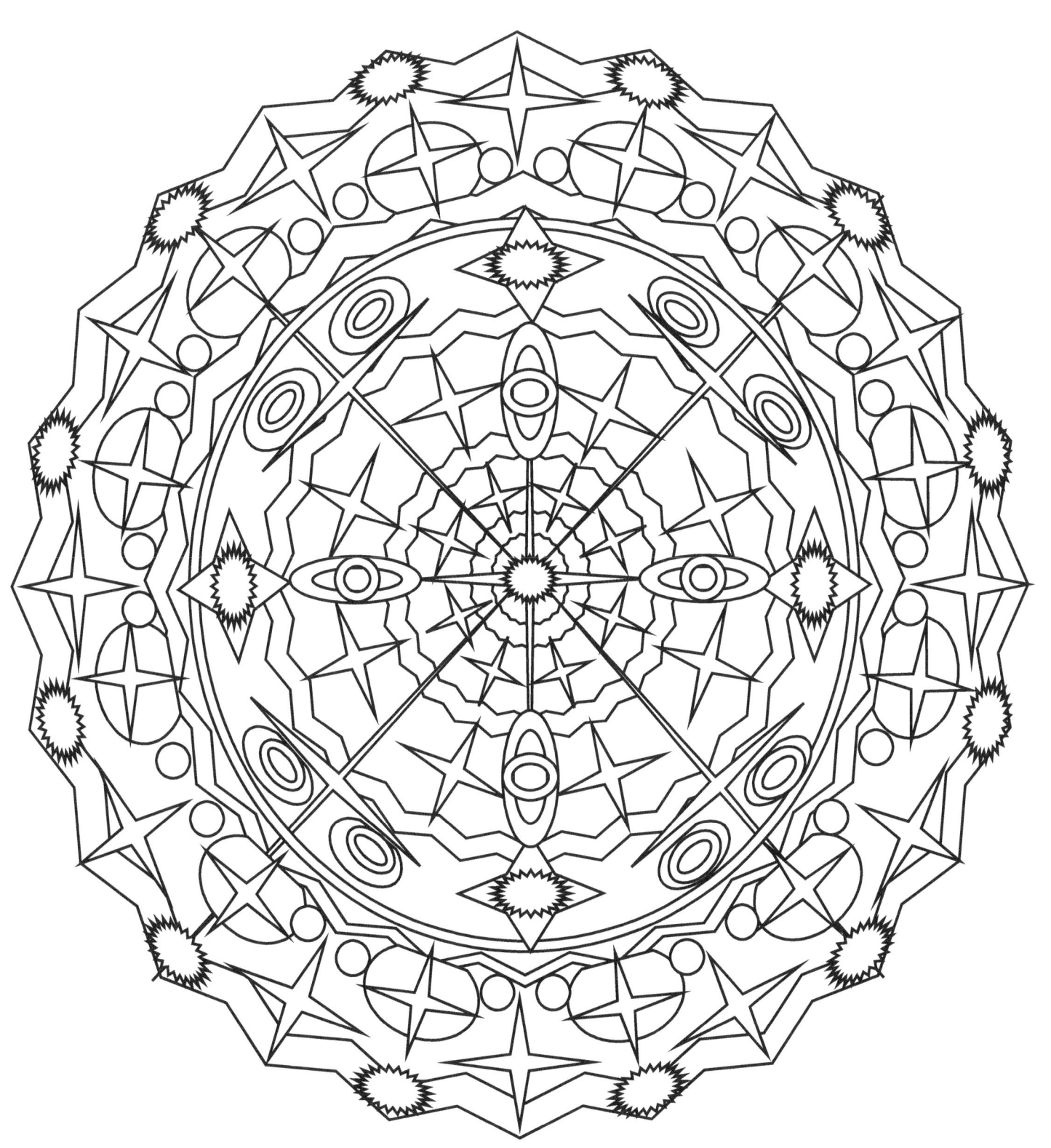

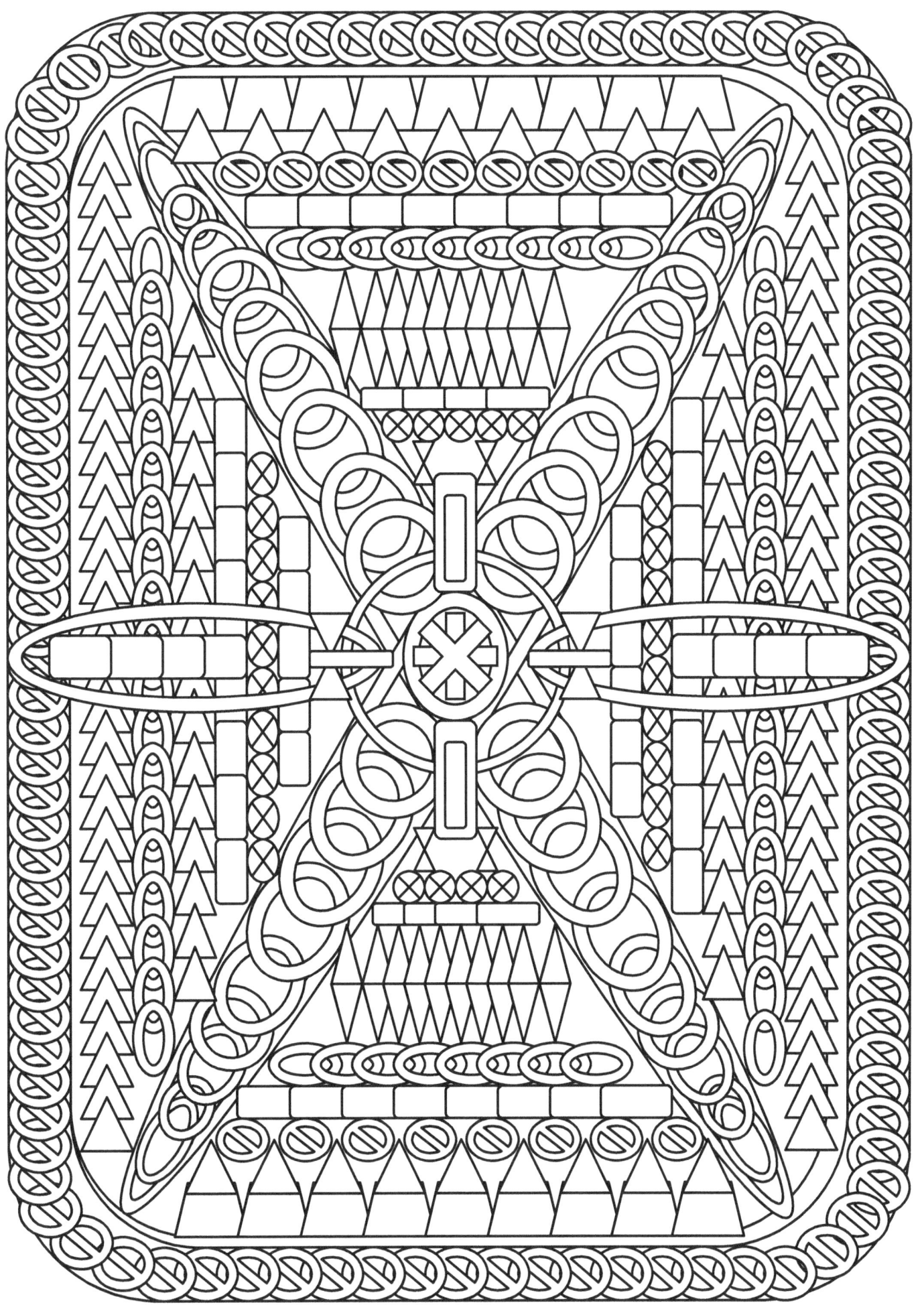

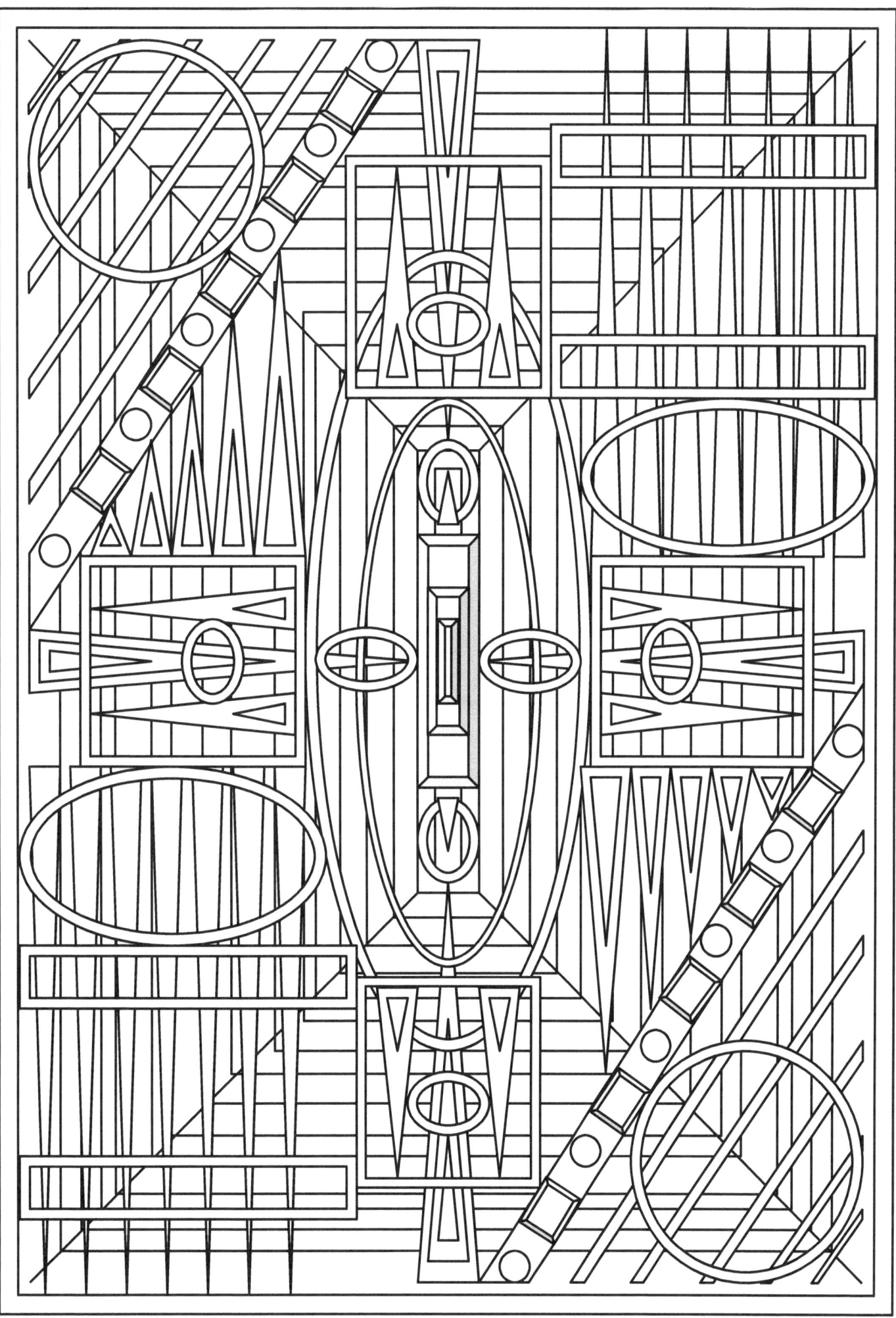

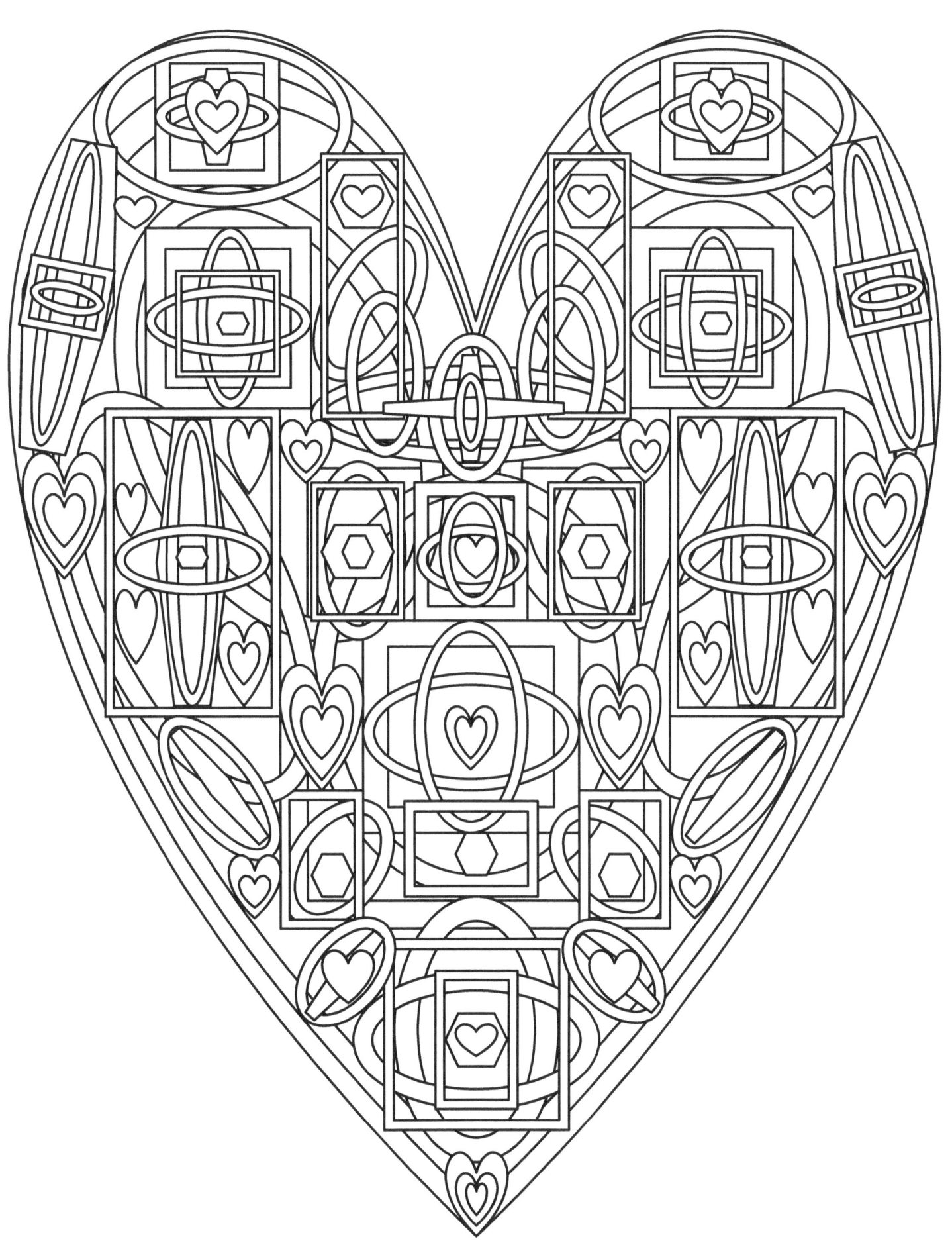

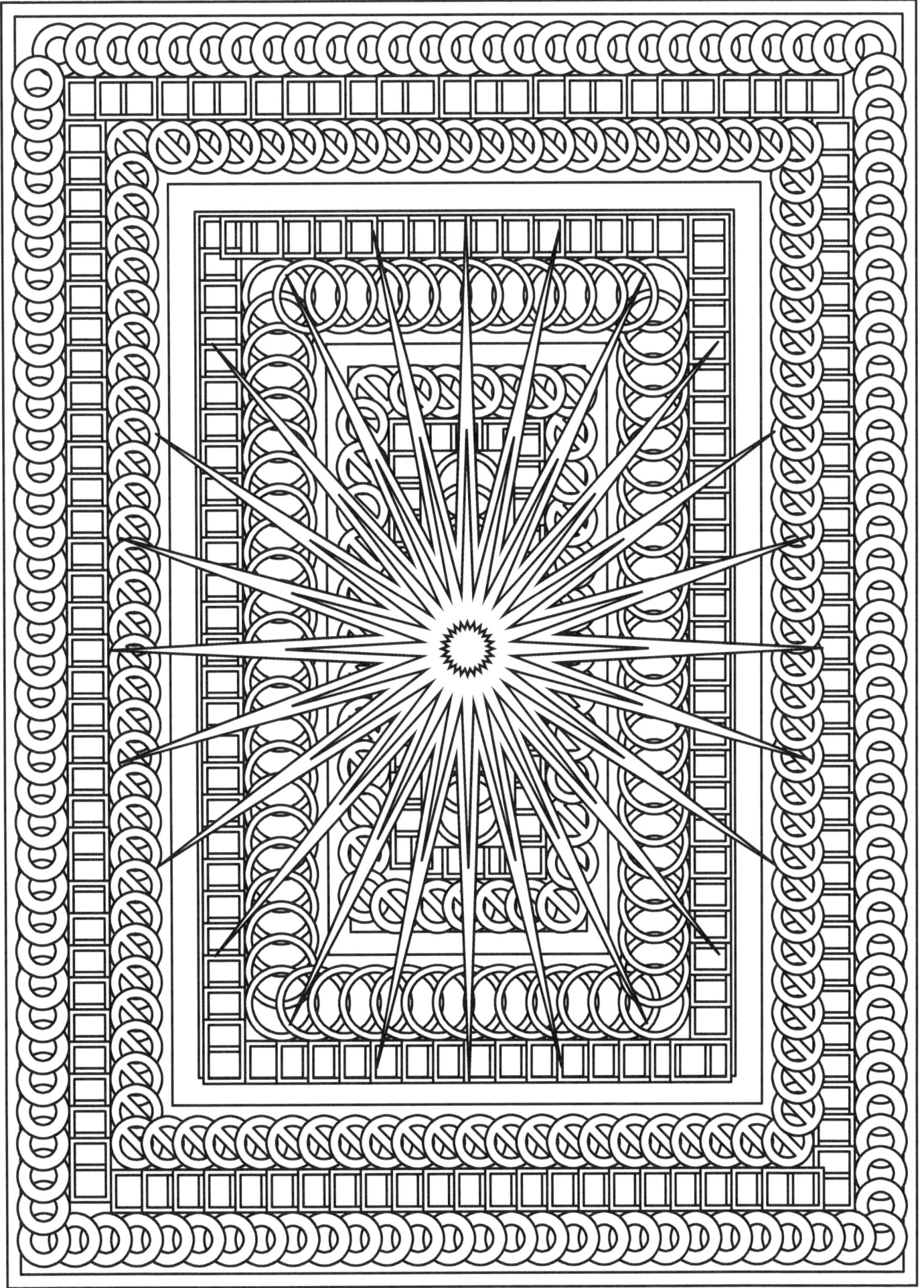

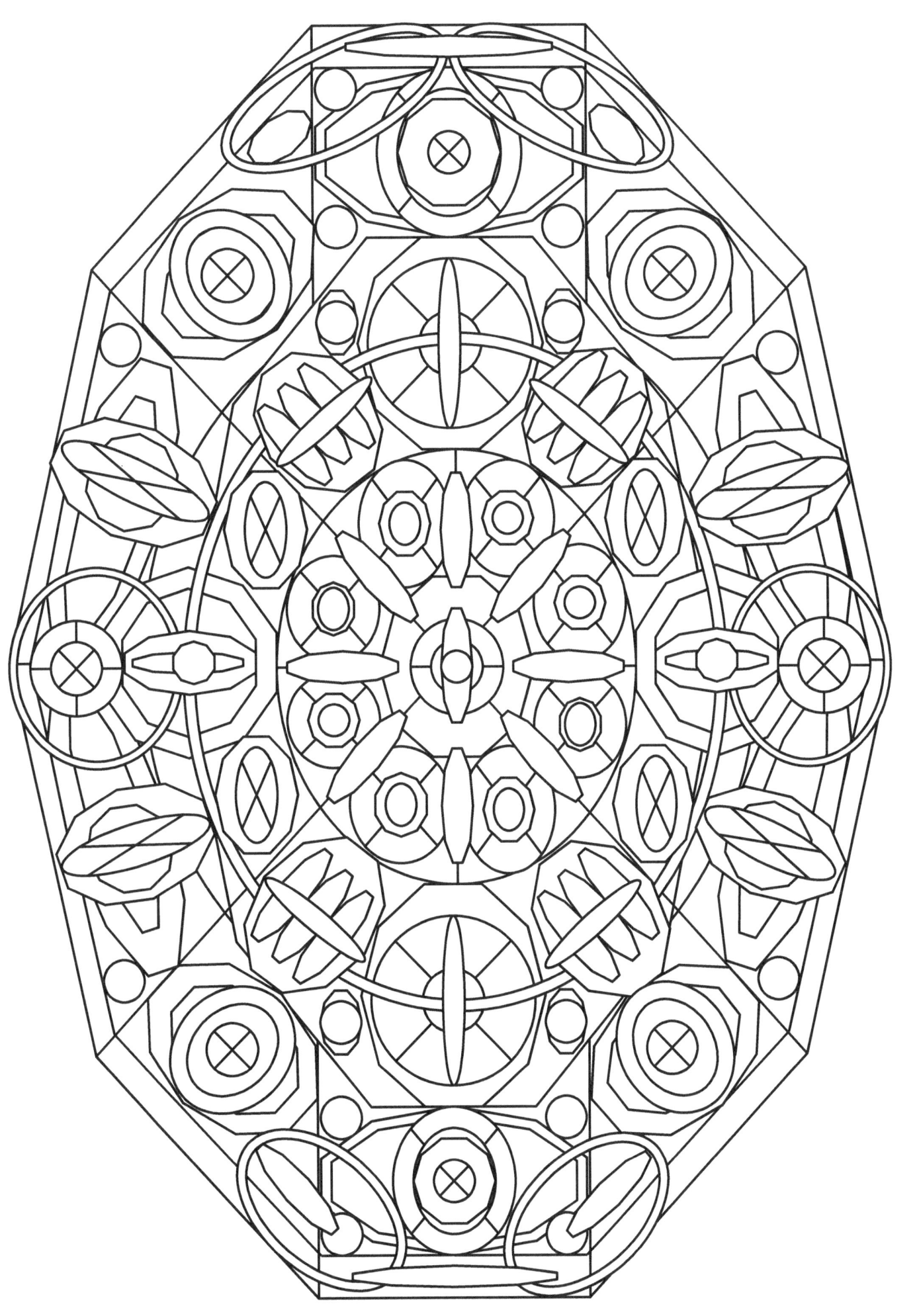

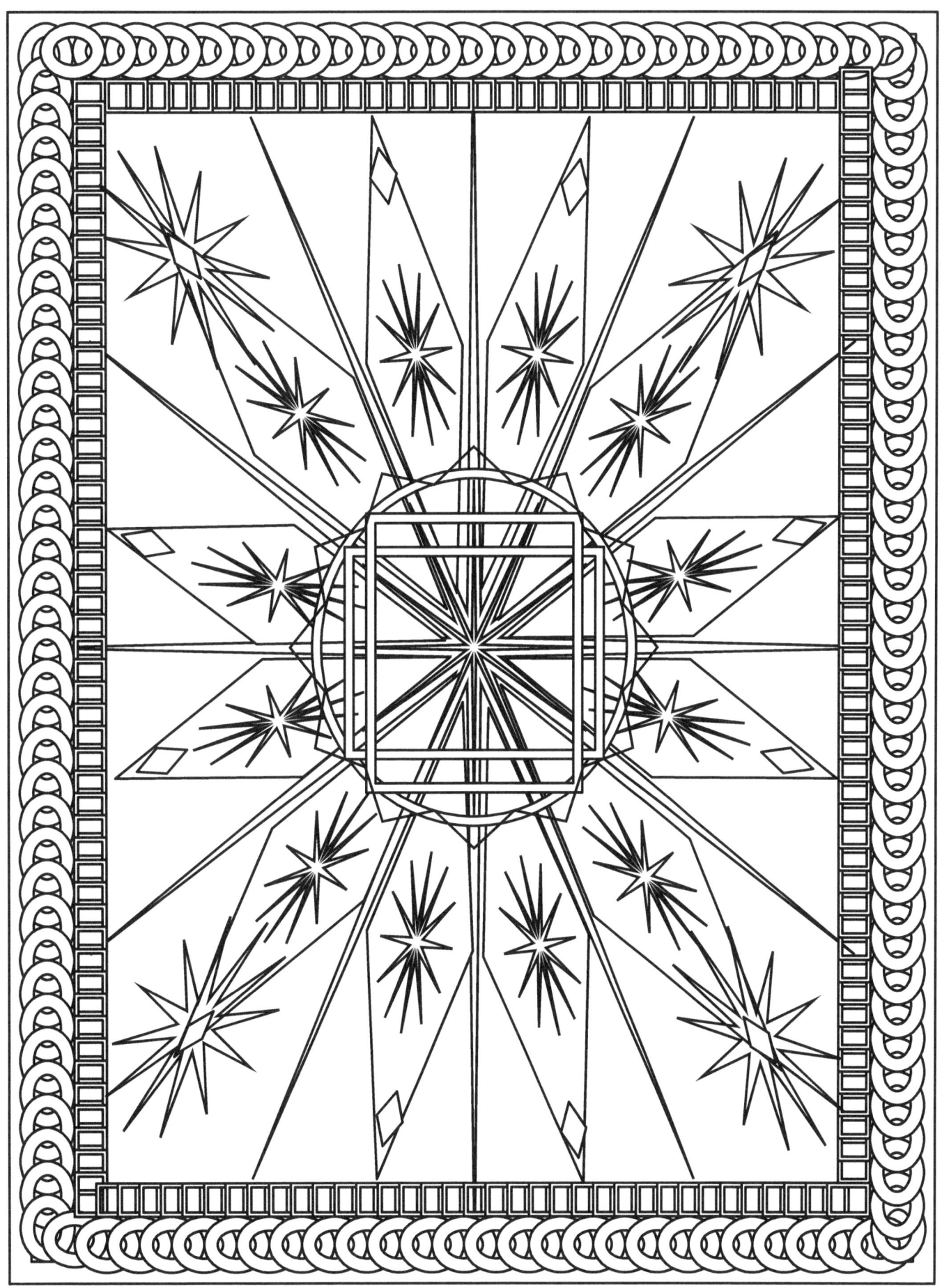

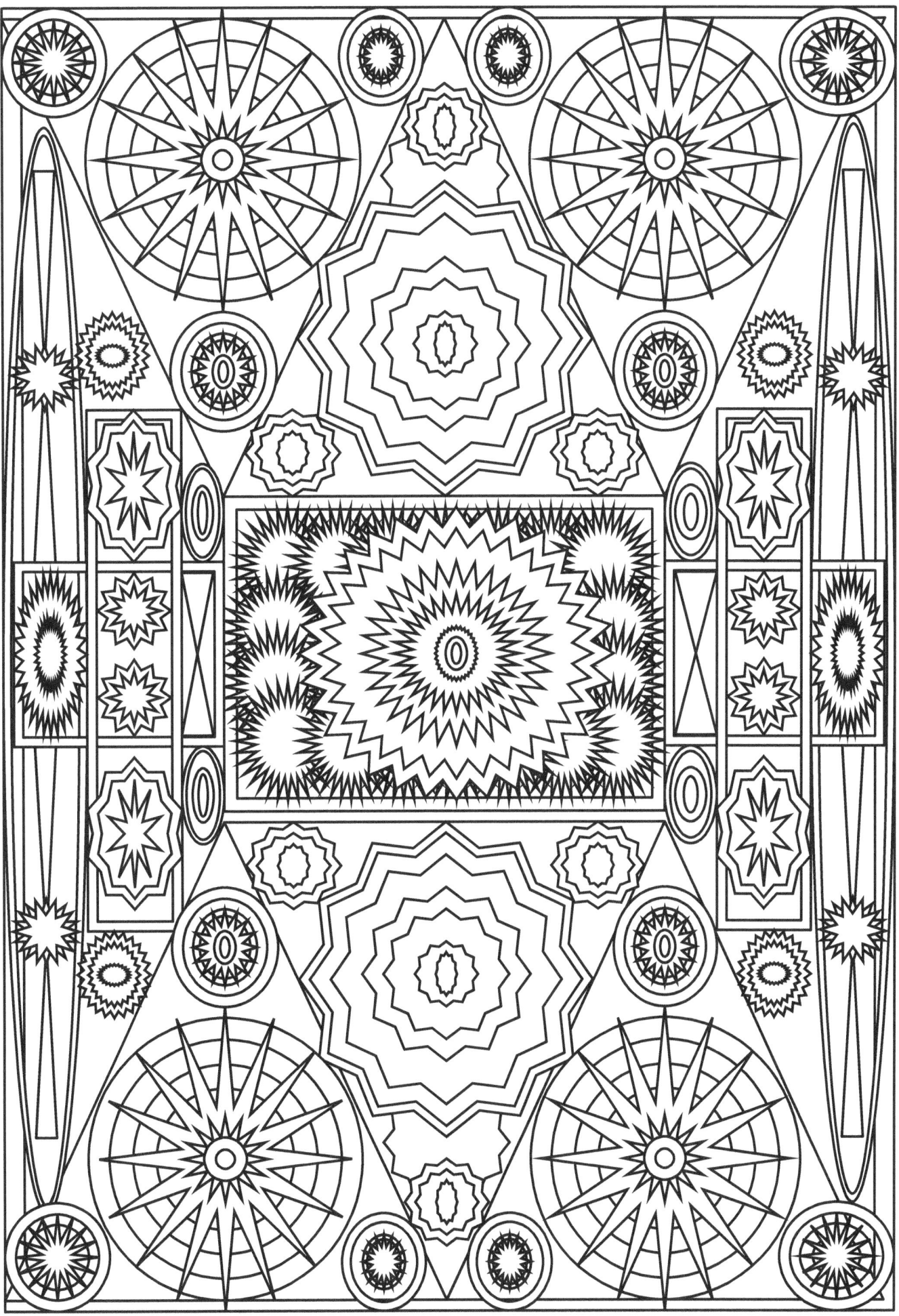

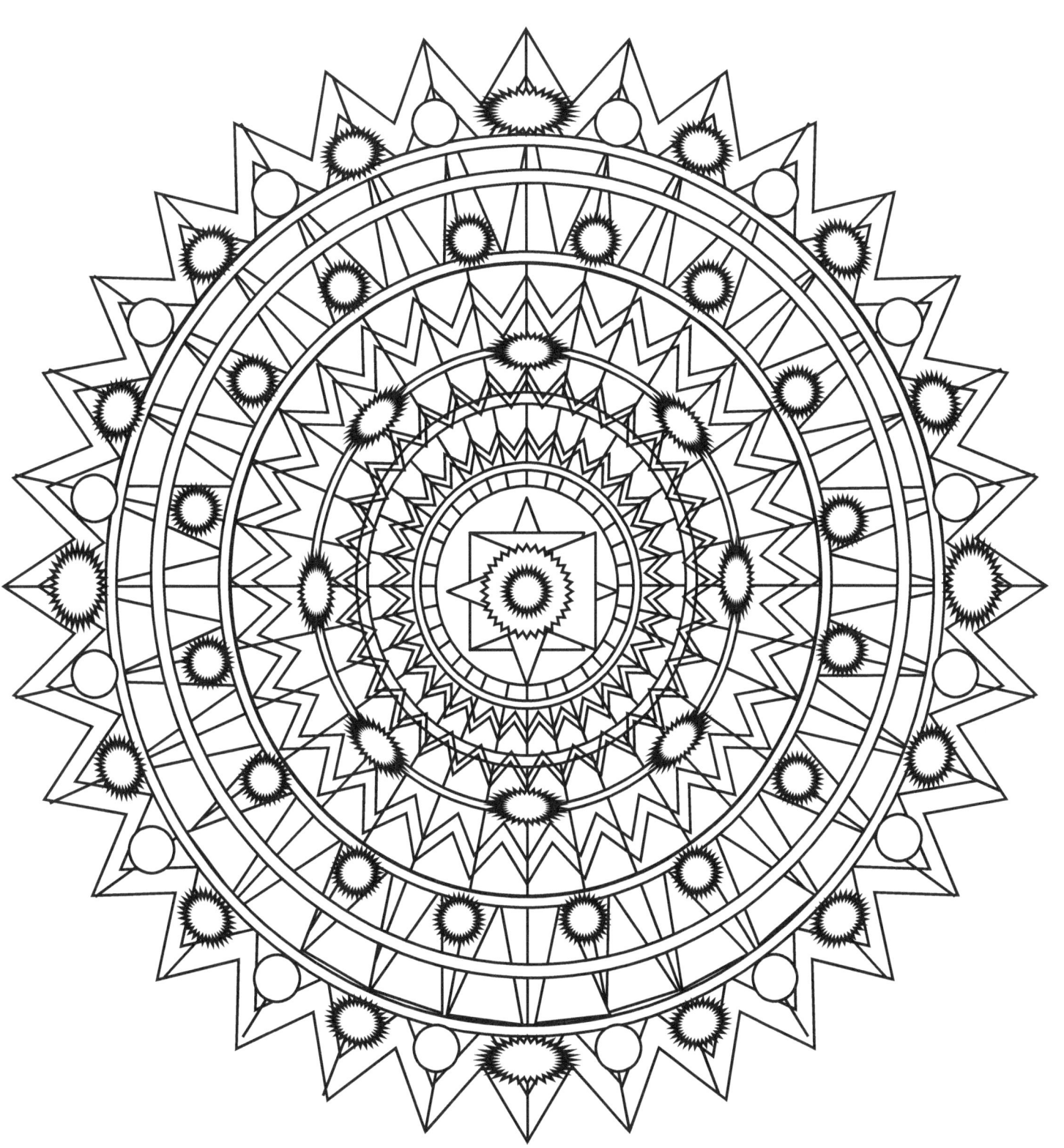

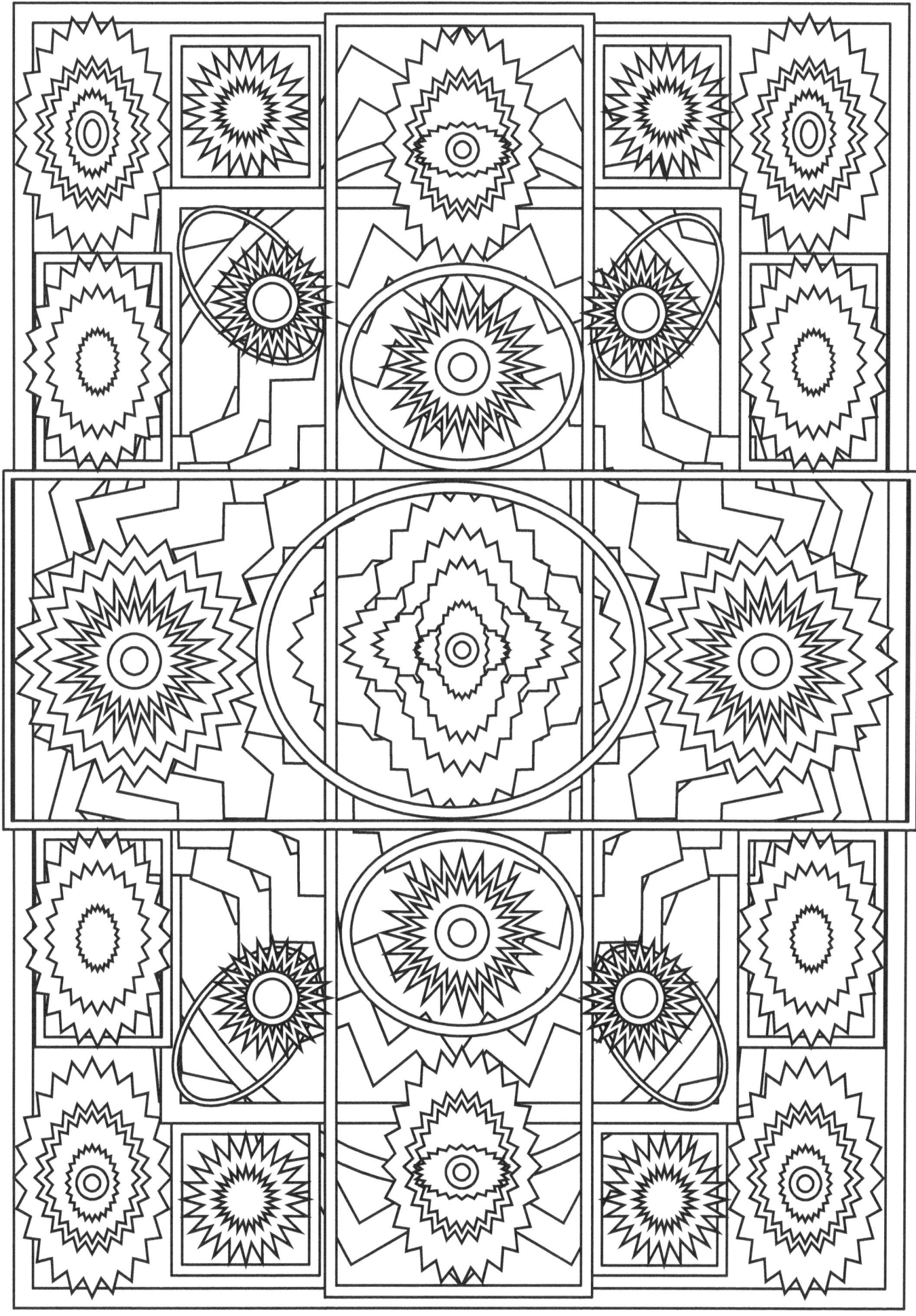

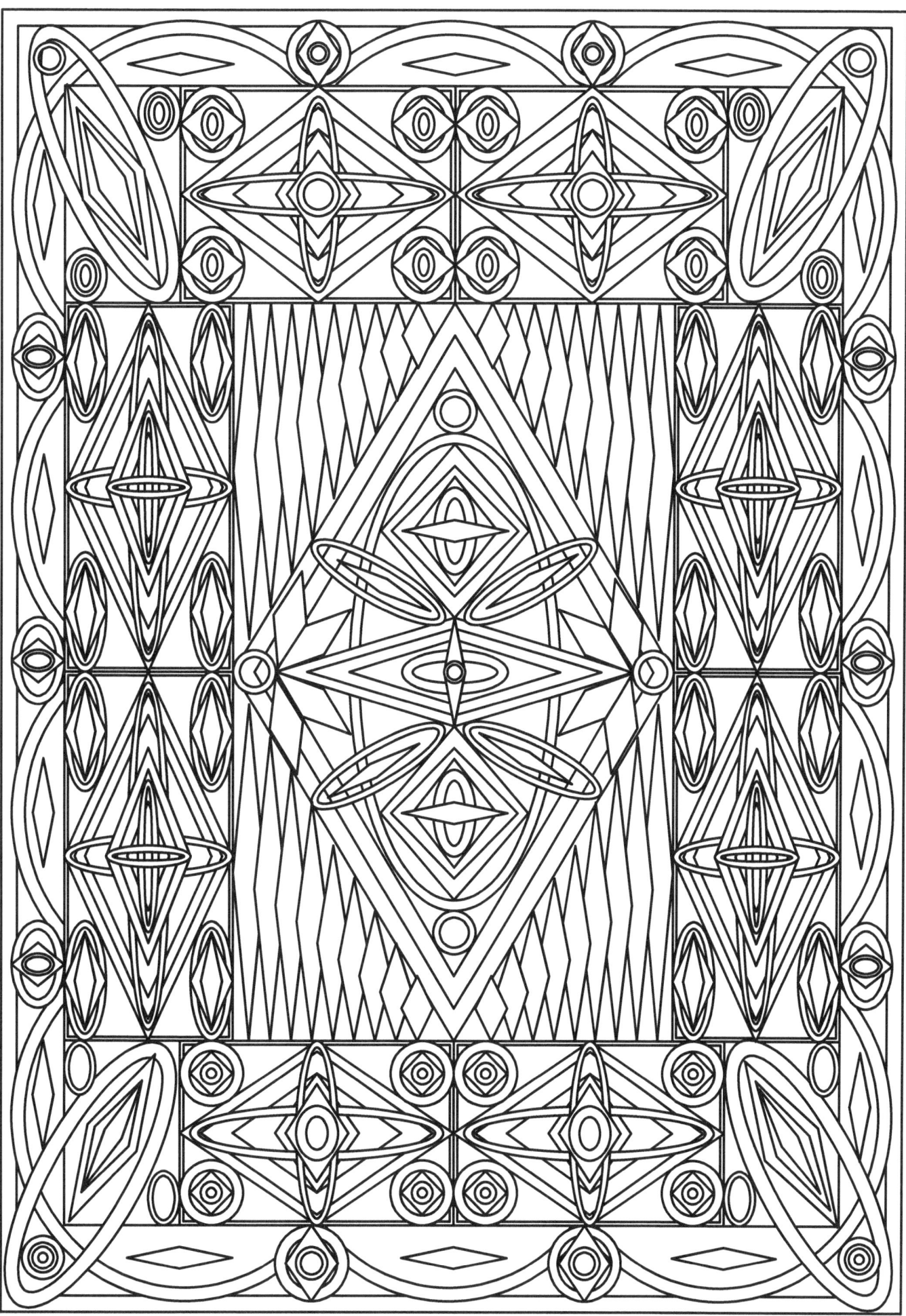

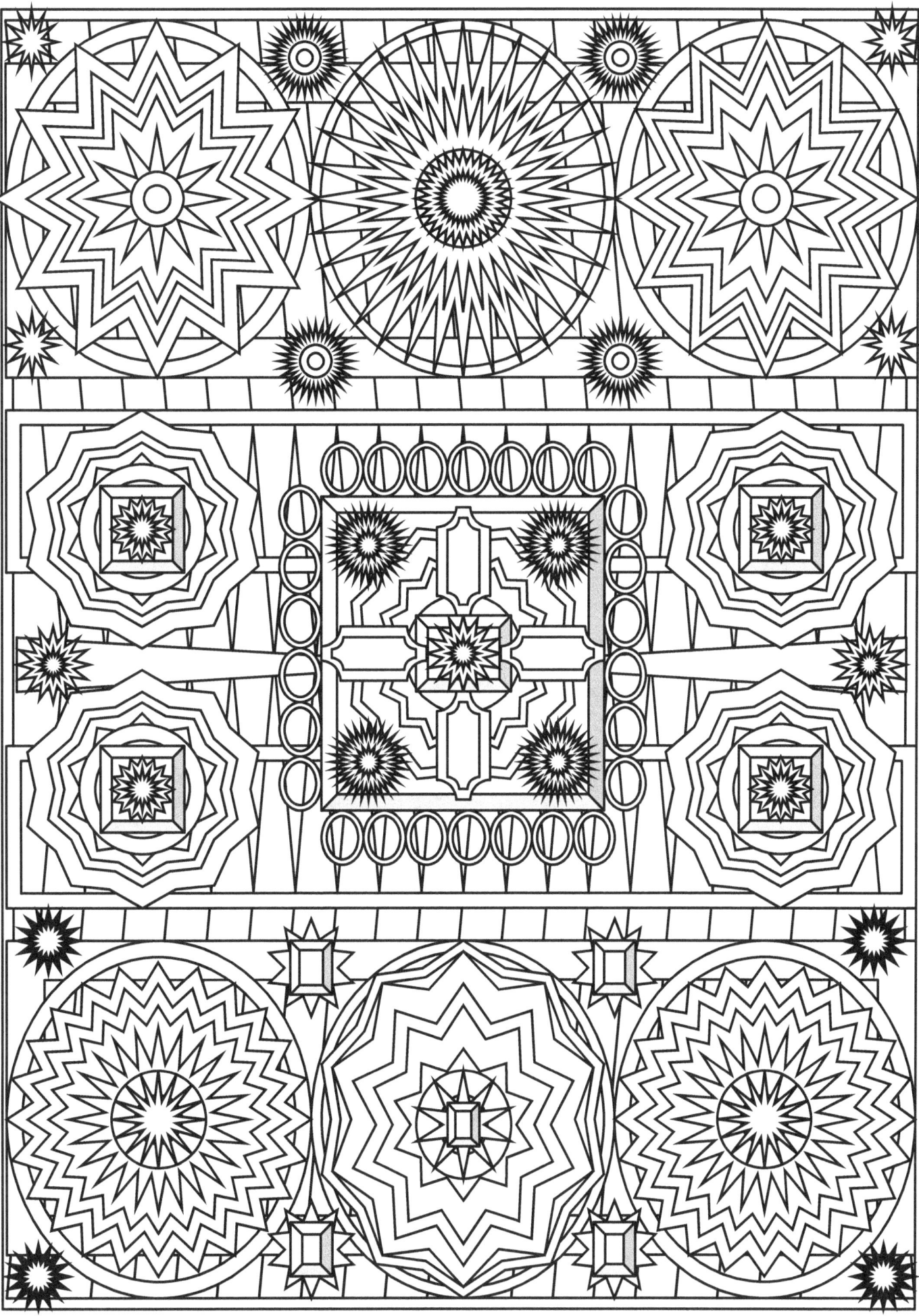

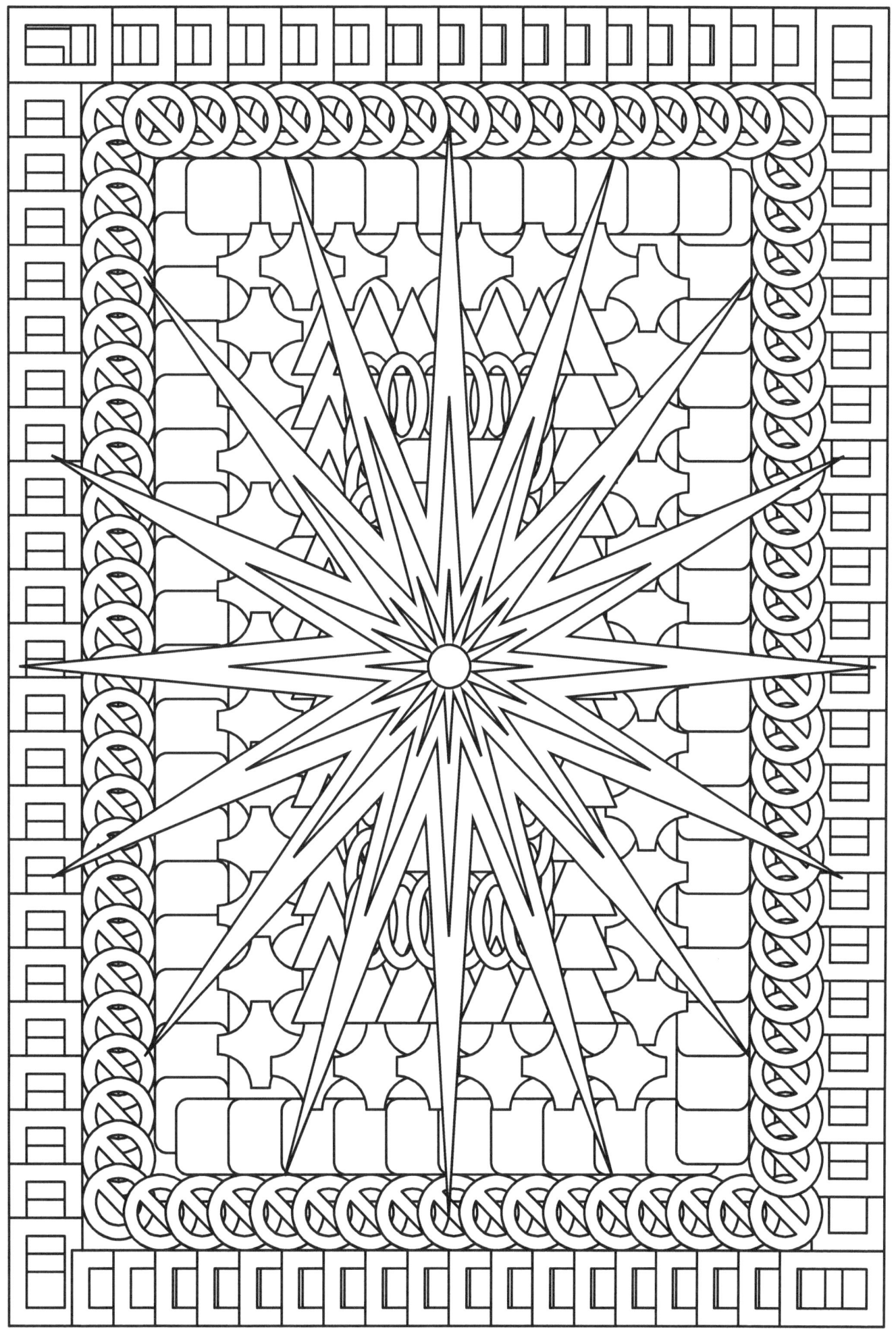

www.ingramcontent.com/pod-product-compliance
Lightning Source LLC
Chambersburg PA
CBHW081307180526
45170CB00007B/2602